NOT A PRIVILEGE.

Bigger is better. No apologies.
Man is at the top of the food chain.

- BBQ ACCORDINGLY -

HARD-CHARGIN'
BLUE CHEESE
STAMPEDE

2	lbs. ground beef		6	ounces blue cheese, cut into 6 pieces
¼	cup chopped onion			
3	Tbsp. Tabasco® sauce		6	hamburger buns, toasted
2	Tbsp. honey			Roasted red peppers (from jar)
1	Tbsp. garlic salt		6	portabella mushrooms, grilled
1	tsp. crushed red pepper flakes			
1	tsp. black pepper			

Preheat grill to medium-high heat. Combine ground beef, onion, Tabasco sauce, honey, garlic salt, red pepper flakes and pepper in a large bowl; mix well. Divide into 6 portions; form into patties around pieces of blue cheese. Grill 8 to 10 minutes or until done. Place burger on bun and top with roasted red peppers and portabella mushrooms.

Makes 6 servings.

BIG OL' MESS

The sloppier it gets, the better it tastes.

1   lb. smoked sausage, cut into chunks
3   jalapeño peppers, sliced
1   green pepper, cut into bite-size chunks
1   sweet onion, cut into bite-size chunks
1   foil cooking bag (see page 36)
¼   cup Tabasco® sauce
1   10-ounce jar sweet-and-sour sauce

Place sausage, peppers and onion in foil bag. Mix Tabasco sauce with sweet-and-sour sauce in a small bowl and pour over the mixture in foil bag; seal edge tightly. Place foil bag on grill; cook for about 45 minutes, turning every 15 minutes. Slit open and serve right out of the bag.

Makes 6 to 8 appetizer servings
or 4 main course servings.

This is great as an appetizer or main dish. To serve, use skewers or load onto chunks of crusty bread.

Where There's Smoke...

Ask 20 BBQers how to start a grill and you'll get 20 different answers. So here are some surefire tips every backyard pit boss can't do without.

- First things first: Always clean your grill grate thoroughly with a wire brush.

- NEVER use gasoline or alcohol to start your fire.

- To use the right amount of charcoal, layer the bottom of the grill with briquettes and then stack in a pyramid. Before lighting, make sure to open the vents on the bottom.

- When the coals are up to heat, spread them out evenly and replace the grill grate.

- With tongs, run a paper towel dabbed in vegetable oil over the grate so your food won't stick.

- Round up your food and your friends— it's time to grill.

GRILLER'S 101

IT ISN'T EVERYTHING THERE IS TO KNOW.
BUT IT'S A DARNED GOOD START.

Know When It's 'Go Time.'

Check out those coals to see if they're up to heat and ready to use.

HIGH: Coals glow red-hot and have a thin white coating of ash (after 20 to 25 minutes).

MEDIUM-HIGH: Coals are barely glowing and have thick ash coating (roughly 30 minutes).

MEDIUM: Coals are solid ash colored (longer than 30 minutes).

GAS GRILLS: Preheat with the lid on for 10-15 minutes and you'll be ready to grill.

The Skinny On Direct And Indirect Heat.

Depending on what the recipe calls for, you'll want to set up your charcoal or gas grill for either direct or indirect heat.

Direct Heat

Cooks food quickly right over the heat. Great for smaller, flatter foods like steaks, burgers and poultry.

Indirect Heat

Cooks food slowly at a lower temperature. Works for bigger foods like ribs, briskets and whole birds. Be sure to place a drip pan under the food.

GETTIN' FANCY
ON THE GRILL
IS LIKE PLAYING
LEAPFROG WITH A UNICORN.
IT NEVER WORKS.

A double dose of chilies gives these ribs a kick.

TWO-TIMING
SHORT RIBS

4 to 5 lbs. beef short ribs, cut into pieces
1   tsp. salt
1   tsp. black pepper
1   12-ounce bottle chili sauce

½   cup beer or orange juice
2   Tbsp. minced onion
2   Tbsp. cider vinegar
2   Tbsp. Worcestershire sauce
1   Tbsp. chili powder
2   tsp. sugar

Sprinkle ribs with salt and pepper.
Combine remaining ingredients in a medium saucepan. Bring to boil over high heat; reduce heat and simmer 5 minutes. Set aside.

Preheat grill to medium-high heat.
Grill ribs for 20 minutes, turning frequently. Baste ribs liberally with sauce and continue to cook another 20 minutes.

Makes 4 servings.

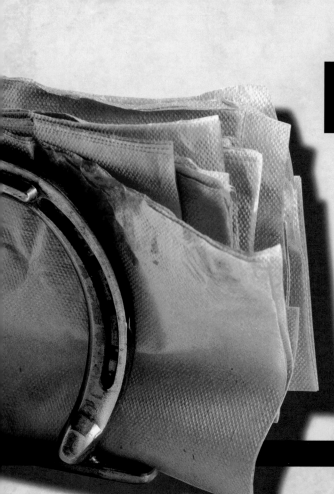

ROADHOUSE
RIBS

3 to 5 lbs. baby back ribs
2 tsp. salt
1 tsp. black pepper
Drip pan (see page 37)

1 cup hoisin sauce
1 cup grape jelly
2 Tbsp. Worcestershire sauce
2 Tbsp. dry mustard
1 Tbsp. light brown sugar
1 tsp. garlic powder
1 tsp. Tabasco® sauce
Juice from 1 lime

Sprinkle ribs with salt and pepper; set aside. Preheat grill for indirect cooking over medium heat (see page 7). Place ribs on grill over drip pan. Cover and cook until tender, about 1 hour.

Meanwhile, combine remaining ingredients in a medium saucepan. Bring to a boil over medium-low heat; reduce heat and simmer 5 minutes. When ribs are tender, move them to direct heat and continue to grill, uncovered. Baste with sauce and turn until crisp on both sides, about 5 minutes. Cut ribs into sections. Serve with remaining sauce.

Makes 4 servings.

THIRSTY BIRD

SPICE RUB MIX:

¼	cup paprika
1	Tbsp. light brown sugar
2	tsp. cayenne pepper
2	tsp. ground cinnamon
2	tsp. dry mustard
1	tsp. garlic powder
1	tsp. onion powder
1	tsp. salt

1	whole chicken, 4 to 5 lbs.
1	12-ounce can beer or non-alcoholic beer
1	Tbsp. fresh lime juice

Mesquite chips (for smoking packet, see page 37)

Drip pan (see page 37)

Mix all ingredients for Spice Rub Mix in a small bowl. Set aside.

Thoroughly clean and rinse chicken. Pat dry. Coat inside and outside of chicken with several tablespoons Spice Rub Mix. Refrigerate at least 1 hour or overnight.

Preheat grill for indirect cooking over medium heat using mesquite chips (see page 7).

Pour out ⅓ of beer from can. Add lime juice to can and place on drip pan in center of grill. Carefully position chicken upright over beer can, adjusting legs to balance. Sprinkle with more Spice Rub Mix. Cook on covered grill 1 hour, or until juices run clear when pierced with fork. (Keep lid closed as much as possible.) Using tongs and oven mitts, carefully remove the chicken and can from the grill. Let chicken rest upright for 10 minutes before lifting from can. Discard beer. Carve chicken or cut into serving pieces.

Makes 4 servings.

IS IT DONE ALREADY?

COOKING A PERFECT STEAK EVERY TIME IS EASY. PICK UP A MEAT THERMOMETER.

★ Get an accurate reading from your instant-read thermometer: Always push it into the thickest part of the meat for 15–20 seconds near the end of suggested grilling time.

(FOR BEEF ONLY) INTERNAL TEMPERATURE

130° **Very Rare** — Red cool center. CHECK TO SEE IF IT'S STILL KICKING.

140° **Rare** — Red center. STILL NOT DONE ENOUGH FOR MOST FOLKS.

145°–150° **Med. Rare** — Red/pink center. NOW YOU'RE TALKIN'.

155°–160° **Med. Done** — Pink center. TEMPERATURE OF CHOICE FOR MOST CARNIVORES.

165° **Med. Well Done** — Light gray center. THERE MIGHT BE A LITTLE TASTE LEFT.

170°–180° **Well Done** — Gray hot center. CHARRED ALMOST BEYOND RECOGNITION.

Note: Meat keeps cooking after you take it off the grill, so remove when it's 5° below desired temperature. Let stand a few minutes before carving and serving.

As for white meat, there's only one way to grill it: Well Done. Cook pork to **155°** and chicken and turkey to **170°**.

FIREWALKER T-BONE

Place steak in bag. Combine remaining ingredients in a small bowl; pour over steak and refrigerate at least 1 hour or overnight. Remove steak from bag and pour marinade into small saucepan. Bring to a boil over low heat and simmer 5 minutes. Reserve half. Use remaining half to baste while grilling, 8 to 10 minutes per side or until done. Pour reserved marinade over meat before serving.

Makes 4 servings.

4	T-bone steaks
	Large resealable plastic bag
½	cup honey
½	cup lime juice
½	cup chopped cilantro
¼	cup Dijon mustard
2	Tbsp. minced canned chipotle peppers in adobo sauce
2	Tbsp. adobo sauce from canned chipotle peppers
6	cloves garlic, minced
1	tsp. ground cumin
1	tsp. salt
½	tsp. ground allspice
½	tsp. black pepper

SALOON
BURGERS

Preheat grill to medium-high heat. Combine ground beef, onion, cilantro, butter, Worcestershire sauce, peppers, garlic, Tabasco sauce and steak seasoning in a large bowl; mix well. Form into 6 patties. Grill 8 to 10 minutes or until done. Grill rolls until toasted. Place burger on roll and top as desired.

Makes 6 servings.

2	lbs. ground beef
¼	cup finely chopped sweet onion
¼	cup chopped cilantro
¼	cup butter, melted
¼	cup Worcestershire sauce
2	medium jalapeño peppers, minced
2	cloves garlic, minced
2	Tbsp. Tabasco® sauce
1	Tbsp. steak seasoning
6	sourdough rolls, split, buttered

TOPPINGS:

2	beefsteak tomatoes, thickly sliced
6	slices Canadian bacon, grilled
6	slices Swiss cheese
6	slices pineapple, grilled
6	Tbsp. mayonnaise

LAST CALL JALAPEÑOS

8   ounces cream cheese, at room temperature
1   Tbsp. Cajun seasoning
2   tsp. garlic powder
15   large fresh jalapeño peppers,
       seeded and sliced lengthwise
15   slices of bacon, cut in half
Toothpicks

Preheat grill to medium heat.
Mix cream cheese, Cajun seasoning
and garlic powder together.
Fill each jalapeño half with cream
cheese mixture. Wrap stuffed jalapeño
with bacon slice and secure with
toothpick. Place on grill and cook
until bacon is done, about 10 minutes.
Remove toothpicks before serving.

Makes 30 appetizers.

> To kick up the flavor even
> more, sprinkle Cajun
> seasoning over wrapped
> jalapeños before grilling.

"SHIRLEY TREATS ME RIGHT EVERY TIME. IF SHE WEREN'T A GRILL, I MIGHT JUST MARRY HER."

— ANONYMOUS

RED HOT MAMA'S
BBQ SAUCE

1½ cups honey
1 cup ketchup
1 6-ounce can tomato paste
2 cloves garlic, minced
2 Tbsp. lemon juice
1 Tbsp. cocoa powder

1 Tbsp. curry powder
1 Tbsp. paprika
1 Tbsp. soy sauce
1 Tbsp. Worcestershire sauce
2 tsp. Tabasco® sauce
1 tsp. cayenne pepper

Combine all ingredients in a medium saucepan.
Bring to a boil over high heat; reduce heat and simmer 20 minutes.
Use with your favorite chicken, ribs or steak recipe.

Makes about 3 cups.

This sauce makes everything taste a whole lot better. Make up a double batch and store in jars. Keeps for about a month in the refrigerator.

JK'S ORIGINAL
WESTERN WINGS

This marinade is also tasty on cut-up chicken and boneless chicken breasts.

5   lbs. chicken wings
Large resealable plastic bag
1   12-ounce jar apricot preserves
1   cup soy sauce
2   cloves garlic, minced
1   Tbsp. fresh ginger, minced
    or 1 tsp. ginger powder

Thoroughly clean and rinse chicken. Pat dry. Cut wings at joint into two pieces and place in bag. Combine remaining ingredients in a medium bowl. Pour over chicken and refrigerate at least 3 hours or overnight.

Preheat grill to medium heat. Remove wings from bag and discard marinade. Grill for 25 minutes, turning once, until skin is crisp and juices run clear.

Makes 8 servings.

FLAVOR UP THAT BBQ

3 EASY WAYS

GIVE IT SOME BITE. ADD SOME KICK. TURN UP THE TWANG.

Hit The Sauce

Doctor up any store-bought bottled BBQ sauce by gradually adding one or more of these ingredients to taste: honey, brown sugar, hot sauce, orange juice, mustard, soy sauce, chili sauce or garlic.

Marinade On The Cheap

Give your food extra flavor for next to nothing: Combine one bottle Italian salad dressing and 1 clove chopped garlic (or lemon juice, to taste) in a large bowl. Place meat or poultry in a large resealable plastic bag and add marinade. Refrigerate for 2 hours before grilling.

Make Mine A Brine

To add flavor to chicken and pork, make a brine. In a large resealable plastic bag, dissolve ¼ cup salt and ½ cup sugar in 1 quart cold water. Add meat and refrigerate for 1 to 2 hours before grilling.

GRILLER'S RULE #87:
NEVER reuse a marinade that soaked raw meat, poultry or fish without boiling it first. Same goes for any sauce that was basted on raw meat while cooking.

SHRIMP SKEWERS

2 lbs. shrimp, uncooked, peeled and deveined, tails on
Large resealable plastic bag
1 onion, finely chopped
1 cup peanut oil
2 Tbsp. Cajun seasoning
1 Tbsp. chopped garlic
2 tsp. cumin
1 tsp. rosemary
1 tsp. thyme
Wood or metal skewers

Place shrimp in bag. Combine remaining ingredients in a small bowl. Pour over shrimp and refrigerate 1 to 2 hours. Preheat grill to medium heat. Remove shrimp from marinade and thread on skewers. Grill 5 to 7 minutes, turning and basting frequently with marinade. Serve hot with Cajun Butter (see below).

Makes 6 to 8 appetizer servings or 4 main course servings.

CAJUN BUTTER

½ lb. (2 sticks) unsalted butter, melted
1 tsp. basil
1 tsp. tarragon
1 tsp. Cajun seasoning
½ tsp. garlic powder
2 to 3 drops Tabasco® sauce

Combine all ingredients in a small bowl.

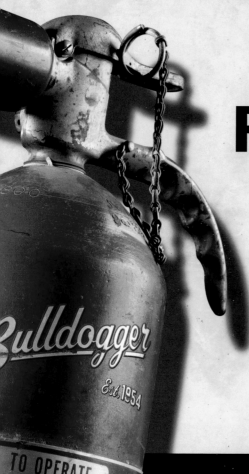

Prepare this side dish ahead of time and refrigerate until ready to grill.

RED HOT
POTATOES & CORN

4	large potatoes, cut into wedges
2	ears of corn, cleaned, cut in half
2	medium onions, peeled, sliced
1	cup hickory-flavored BBQ sauce
¼	cup butter or margarine, sliced into 8 pieces
¼	cup Tabasco® green jalapeño sauce
4	cloves garlic, peeled, sliced
1	large foil cooking bag (see page 36)

Preheat grill to medium-high heat. Combine all ingredients in a large bowl, stir to coat. Transfer ingredients to foil bag and seal edge tightly. Place on grill and cover, turning every 10 minutes. Remove when potatoes are soft, about 20 minutes. Serve with additional jalapeño and BBQ sauce, if desired.

Makes 4 servings.

EMPTY OUT THE ICEBOX
BBQ PIZZA

1 lb. ready-made pizza dough,
   at room temperature
2 Tbsp. olive oil
½ lb. cooked sausage, cut into
   ½-inch pieces
1 cup assorted grilled vegetables
   (peppers, onions, zucchini, mushrooms)
6 ounces shredded Colby jack cheese
1 tsp. basil
¼ tsp. dry red pepper flakes

Preheat grill to medium-high heat. Oil grill rack (see page 6).

Roll out dough to a 12"x 15" rectangle. Brush top with olive oil. Place dough, oil side down, on grill rack. Cover and grill about 3 minutes, or until bottom is lightly browned. Punch down air bubbles, if needed. Brush top with olive oil and turn over. Immediately top evenly with remaining ingredients. Cover and cook 3 minutes or until cheese is melted.

Makes 4 servings.

Make it your own: Follow the recipe to grill up the pizza crust, and then load on your favorite toppings.

BARELY OVER THE BORDER

FAJITAS

2 lbs. flank or skirt steak	Juice of 1 lime	1 tsp. salt
Large resealable plastic bag	1 tsp. garlic powder	Mesquite chips
½ cup balsamic vinegar or red wine vinegar	1 tsp. chipotle pepper powder or chili powder	(for smoking packet, see page 37)
⅓ cup olive oil		Flour tortillas
⅓ cup tequila or lemon juice	1 tsp. onion powder	Grilled onions and peppers
		Pico de gallo

Place steak in bag. Mix vinegar, olive oil, tequila, lime juice, garlic powder, chipotle pepper powder, onion powder and salt in a small bowl. Pour over steak. Refrigerate at least 1 hour or overnight.

Preheat grill to medium-high heat using mesquite chips. Remove steak from bag; grill 8 to 10 minutes per side or until done. Remove and let meat rest several minutes; slice into strips. Serve with grilled flour tortillas, grilled onions and peppers and pico de gallo.

Makes 4 to 6 servings.

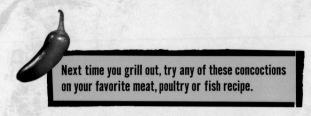

Next time you grill out, try any of these concoctions on your favorite meat, poultry or fish recipe.

SWEET & SMOKY RUB

2	cups light brown sugar	1	Tbsp. garlic salt
2	Tbsp. paprika	1	Tbsp. lemon pepper
2	Tbsp. chili powder	2	Tbsp. liquid smoke
2	Tbsp. seasoned salt		

Combine all ingredients in a medium bowl; mix well.
Spread out on a cookie sheet to dry, about 2 to 3 hours.
To use, rub into meat and refrigerate at least 2 hours
or overnight. Grill or cook as desired.
Keeps in a covered container for up to 1 month.

Makes about 2½ cups.

TEAR JERKER MARINADE

½ lb. jalapeño peppers, chopped
1 medium yellow onion, chopped
1 cup cilantro leaves
1 16-ounce can crushed pineapple
½ cup teriyaki sauce
Juice from 1 lime or 2 Tbsp. lime juice
2 tsp. salt

Combine all ingredients in
blender; blend about 2 minutes,
or until mixture is finely pureed.
Pour into jars and refrigerate at least
5 hours. To use as marinade, pour over
any meat and refrigerate several hours or
overnight. Can also be used as a basting sauce
while grilling. Keeps in refrigerator 1 week.

Makes about 3½ cups.

HORN–HONKIN'
BBQ SAUCE

1	cup ketchup		¼	cup red wine vinegar
½	cup beer or non-alcoholic beer		¼	cup Worcestershire sauce
			1	Tbsp. steak seasoning
½	cup light brown sugar		2	tsp. garlic powder
½	cup finely chopped onion		1	tsp. Cajun seasoning

Combine all ingredients in a medium saucepan. Bring to a boil over high heat; reduce heat and simmer 10 minutes. Use as a basting sauce while grilling.

Makes about 3½ cups.

ALUMINUM FOIL
the griller's sidekick

4 GREAT TIPS

IT CLEANS.
IT SMOKES.
IT EVEN MAKES A GREAT TV ANTENNA.

Foil Bags: Grillin' Without The Mess.

Using a foil bag is as easy as making one. Start by tearing off a 12" x 18" sheet of heavy-duty foil. Place meat, veggies and sides on foil and season to taste. Cover with a second sheet; fold and crimp the edges. Normal cooking times apply — minus the clean-up.

Turn Your Grill Into A BBQ Smoker.

Soak a handful of wood chips (like hickory or mesquite) in water for an hour. Remove the chips and mound up on a sheet of heavy-duty foil. Fold the foil over and crimp the edges. Poke 3 or 4 holes in the top ONLY. When grill is up to heat, place the packet directly on the coals and you're ready to roll.

Spend Time Grilling. Not Cleaning.

Check out these quick cleaning tips using foil: If you don't have a wire brush, crumple a sheet of foil into a ball and run it over the grate. Or, when you're done grilling, place a sheet of foil over the grate while it's still hot. Any odds and ends left behind will burn right up.

Avoid Flare-Ups. Make A Drip Pan.

Catch the fat that runs off whole chickens and ribs. Pick up a disposable drip pan at the supermarket, or make one out of heavy-duty foil by tearing off a 12" x 14" sheet and folding in the edges 1". Then fold edges upright. At the corners, pinch the foil diagonally and press along sides. Place under your food and next to charcoal when using indirect heat (see page 7).

"IF IT WEREN'T FOR **BBQ-ING,** I'D HAVE NO REASON TO HAVE **A BACKYARD.**"

— Willy Hawk

CLASSIC BACKYARD
BEER BRATS

2   12-ounce cans beer
      or non-alcoholic beer
2   tsp. sugar
½   tsp. black pepper
Disposable foil pan
10   fresh bratwurst
3   onions, sliced
2   Tbsp. vegetable oil
10   rolls or hot dog buns, toasted

Preheat grill for indirect cooking over medium-high heat (see page 7). Mix beer, sugar and pepper in a foil pan centered on grate. Brush brats and onion slices with oil and grill over coals on either side of foil pan until nicely browned, turning once. Place brats and onion slices in the beer mixture, cover pan with foil and continue cooking for 20 to 30 minutes longer.

Serve brats and onions on rolls with your favorite condiments.

Makes 10 servings.

AUTHENTIC WESTERN WILD
BURGERS

1½ lbs. ground venison, elk, buffalo or bison (choose one)

1 lb. hot bulk pork sausage

1 medium onion, finely chopped

5 cloves garlic, finely chopped

1 habanero pepper, finely chopped

¼ cup Tabasco® sauce

¼ cup Worcestershire sauce

2 Tbsp. oregano

2 tsp. seasoned salt

½ tsp. cayenne pepper

4 hamburger buns, toasted

Combine all ingredients in a large bowl and refrigerate several hours. Preheat grill to medium-high heat. Form meat into 4 patties, grill 8 to 10 minutes or until done. Place burger on bun and top as desired.

Makes 4 servings.

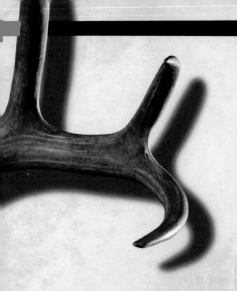

BLAZIN'
VENISON STEAKS

4 to 6 venison steaks	3 cloves garlic, chopped
4 to 6 portabella mushrooms	½ tsp. salt
1 Tbsp. vegetable oil	¼ cup red wine or water
4 habanero peppers, chopped	1 tsp. dry mustard
¼ cup Worcestershire sauce	1 tsp. ground cinnamon

Place steaks in a baking dish. Arrange portabellas on top of steaks. Set aside.

In a small skillet, heat oil and cook habaneros until softened. Add Worcestershire sauce, garlic and salt; heat until sizzling. Remove from heat. Add wine, mustard and cinnamon; stir until blended. Pour over steaks and portabellas, cover and refrigerate at least 1 hour or overnight.

Preheat grill to medium-high heat. Remove steaks and portabellas from marinade and place on grill. Using marinade to baste, grill portabellas about 15 minutes; grill steaks 6 to 7 minutes, turning once, until done.

Makes 4 to 6 servings.

Can't find wild game at the supermarket? Try your local butcher shop or specialty food store.

SAUCE:

¼   cup butter
2   cups chopped onion
2   cups ketchup
2   cups BBQ sauce
1   12-ounce can beer
    or 1½ cups water
¼   cup light brown sugar
2   Tbsp. chili powder
2   Tbsp. ground cinnamon
2   Tbsp. Worcestershire sauce
1   Tbsp. prepared mustard
1   Tbsp. vinegar

Heat butter in a large saucepan. Add onion and stir frequently until softened, about 5 minutes. Add remaining ingredients; simmer over low heat for 30 minutes.

DOWN HOME
PULLED PORK

5   lbs. boneless pork loin   1   Tbsp. garlic salt
1   Tbsp. black pepper   8 to 10 rolls or hamburger buns

Preheat grill for indirect cooking over medium heat (see page 7). Sprinkle pork loin with pepper and garlic salt. Place on grill and cook about 1½ to 2 hours or until internal temperature reaches 155° to 160°. Allow meat to cool while preparing sauce (recipe at left). Shred pork into small pieces, discarding any remaining fat. Place pork in a large pot; stir sauce into pork and simmer 40 minutes. Serve on warmed rolls.

Makes 8 to 10 servings.

HEAT-SEEKING
SWORDFISH STEAKS

3 Tbsp. olive oil, divided	
¼ cup diced onion	
2 cloves garlic, minced	
3 tomatoes, seeded and chopped	1 tsp. Tabasco® sauce
¼ cup chopped black or green olives	½ tsp. salt
2 Tbsp. vinegar	¼ tsp. crushed red pepper flakes
1 Tbsp. capers, chopped	4 swordfish steaks, about
2 tsp. fresh thyme (or 1 tsp. dried)	6 ounces each and 1 inch thick

Heat 2 tablespoons of olive oil in a small saucepan over medium-low heat. Add onion and garlic; cook, stirring often, for 3 minutes or until softened. Add remaining ingredients, except swordfish steaks, and cook 5 minutes longer; set aside until serving time.

Preheat grill to medium-high heat. Brush both sides of swordfish steaks with remaining olive oil and season with salt and red pepper. Place on grill and cook 8 to 10 minutes, turning once, until cooked through. Serve swordfish with sauce spooned over top.

Makes 4 servings.

SPICY FLATTENED
CHICKEN

1	whole chicken, 4 to 5 lbs.	6	tomatillos, cut in half	6	ounces olive oil
	Large resealable plastic bag	6	ounces tequila, optional	1	Tbsp. chili powder
6	jalapeño peppers, seeds removed	6	ounces lime juice	1	tsp. salt
				1	tsp. black pepper

Thoroughly clean and rinse chicken. Pat dry. To remove backbone of chicken, place chicken breast-side down on cutting board and cut along each side of the backbone; discard bone. Open chicken, pressing down on the breastbone to flatten. Place chicken in bag; set aside.

Mix remaining ingredients in blender; reserve 1 cup sauce. Pour remaining sauce over chicken and refrigerate at least 2 hours or overnight.

Preheat grill to medium heat. Remove chicken from bag and discard marinade.
Grill bone-side down for 15 minutes. Turn chicken and cook about 15 minutes more, or until juices run clear when pierced with fork. Serve with reserved sauce.

Makes 4 servings.

CALLING ALL CARNIVORES

GRILLING BEEF IS LIKE CHECKING OUT A MONSTER TRUCK. THERE'S ALWAYS LOTS OF DROOLING.

Bang For The Buck

Don't want to spend a fortune on a tenderloin? Make tougher cuts like flank steak and round tip more flavorful by marinating them before grilling (see "Marinade On The Cheap," page 27).

Serve It Up Right

Before carving and serving, let grilled steaks stand for 2 to 3 minutes. The juices at the center will work their way throughout the meat (for more tips, see page 15).

Put It On Ice

When meat goes on sale, stock up and freeze it. If you're going to use it within 2 weeks, keep it store-wrapped. For longer storage, rewrap it in plastic wrap and foil. Also, always thaw out frozen meat in the fridge—NEVER at room temperature.

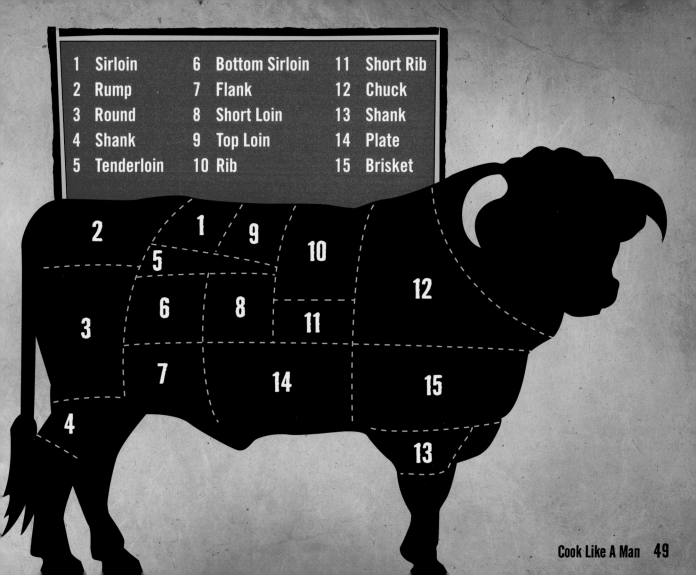

IF YOUR FACE AND HANDS
DON'T GET MESSY
EATING BBQ,
YOU'RE DOING IT
ALL WRONG.

HIGH COUNTRY
BBQ BEANS

1   15-ounce can pork and beans
1   15-ounce can pink beans, rinsed, drained
1   15-ounce can kidney beans, rinsed, drained
½   lb. bacon, cooked, chopped
2   cups smoked ham, chopped

1   large green pepper, chopped
1   large yellow onion, chopped
1   small green chili pepper, chopped
1   cup light brown sugar
½   cup BBQ sauce
2 or 3 cloves garlic, chopped

Preheat grill to medium heat. Combine all ingredients in a large pot; mix well. Simmer covered for several hours; stir often. Remove from heat when vegetables are soft.

Makes 8 servings.

This is an easy one-pot meal to cook while camping. Prepare ahead of time, and cook in a kettle or Dutch oven over the lowest part of the campfire.

MEMPHIS-STYLE
PORK RIBS

To make rub, combine paprika, black pepper, brown sugar, salt, celery salt, cayenne pepper, dry mustard, garlic powder and cumin in a small bowl. Rub two-thirds of the mixture over all surfaces of ribs. Place ribs in a large pan or baking dish, cover and refrigerate at least 4 hours or overnight.

Preheat grill for indirect cooking over medium heat (see page 7). To make mop sauce, whisk together mustard, vinegar and salt in a small bowl; set aside. Arrange ribs on grill. Close lid and cook for 1 hour. Baste with the mop sauce. Cook 30 minutes longer, basting frequently. Remainder of rub can be sprinkled on at the end of cooking, if desired.

Makes 4 to 6 servings.

¼ cup paprika
1½ Tbsp. freshly ground black pepper
1½ Tbsp. firmly packed dark brown sugar
1 Tbsp. salt
1½ tsp. celery salt
1½ tsp. cayenne pepper
1½ tsp. dry mustard
1½ tsp. garlic powder
1½ tsp. ground cumin
4 to 6 lbs. pork ribs

MOP SAUCE:
¼ cup prepared mustard
1 cup cider vinegar
1 tsp. salt

TALK A GOOD GAME.
AND LET YOUR BBQ BACK YOU UP.

Barbeque ("BBQ", "Que"): Although true barbeque is cooked by the "smoking" method, most folks say they're "barbequing" when they're actually "grilling."

Brine: A solution of salt, sugar and water that marinates food before cooking (see page 27). Adds loads of flavor.

Cowboy Barbeque: Texas-style grilling and smoking method. Start by grilling the meat over hot coals until rare, then finish slow-cooking over indirect heat with mesquite chips.

Direct Heat: Cooking food quickly by placing it directly over the heat source (see page 7).

Indirect Heat: Cooking food slowly by not placing it directly over the heat source (see page 7).

Marinade: A flavorful liquid concoction that food soaks in before cooking.

Ms. White: The moist, meaty inside of pork barbeque.

Mister Brown: The dark, smoked outer part of pork barbeque.

Mop Sauce: A mixture basted on food during cooking to add moisture and flavor.

Pachanga: South Texan term for a get-together, complete with BBQ and live music.

Pig Pickin': North Carolina slang for an outdoor gathering where pulled pork is served.

Pitmaster: The craftsman who tends the barbeque pit (or smoker) for hours on end until the meat is perfectly done. The true definition of patience.

Rub: Dry seasonings that are massaged into meat before cooking. Rubs lock in flavor, add a little bite and create a crust on the meat.

Searing: Cooking meat on high heat for a short time. Seals in juices and creates a crunchy outside.

Smoking: Cooking meat for long periods of time at low temperatures. Fired by burning hardwoods that infuse a 'smoky' taste into the meat.

BBQ SAUCE:

- 1   16-ounce can tomato sauce
- 1   12-ounce bottle ketchup
- 1   12-ounce can beer
      or non-alcoholic beer
- ½ cup butter
- ¼ cup Worcestershire sauce
- 1   onion, finely chopped

Juice from 2 limes

- 1   Tbsp. chili powder
- 1   Tbsp. Tabasco® sauce,
      or to taste
- 1   Tbsp. prepared mustard

Combine all ingredients in a medium saucepan. Bring to a boil over medium-low heat; reduce heat and simmer 15 to 20 minutes.

- 1   trimmed brisket, about 6 lbs.
- 1   14-ounce jar sliced jalapeño peppers, reserve juice

Garlic salt and black
     pepper to taste
- 2   large onions, sliced

Preheat grill for indirect cooking over medium heat (see page 7). Prepare brisket by placing in a large pan and poking about 40 holes in each side with fork. Season with garlic salt and black pepper. Pour juice from peppers on each side of brisket. Cover pan with heavy-duty aluminum foil and cook indirectly for about 1½ to 2 hours.

On a large double layer of heavy-duty foil, place ½ of the onions and ½ jar of jalapeño pepper slices. Remove brisket from grill and lay it on top of the onions and peppers. Brush brisket with ⅓ cup BBQ sauce (recipe at left). Top with remaining onions and peppers and wrap tightly in foil. Place on the grill and cook indirectly another 1 to 2 hours. Remove from the grill and unwrap. To serve, cut into thin slices against the grain. Serve with remaining sauce.

Makes 8 to 10 servings.

PRAIRIE FIRE
BEEF BRISKET

FOOT-STOMPIN'
FIRE-BREATHIN' CHICKEN

2 lbs. chicken pieces
Large resealable plastic bag
1 cup cola
2 jalapeño peppers,
   seeds removed, pureed
   or finely chopped
2 Tbsp. light brown sugar
1 tsp. seafood seasoning

Thoroughly clean and rinse chicken pieces. Pat dry. Place chicken in bag. Combine remaining ingredients in a medium bowl; reserve 1/4 cup marinade. Pour remaining marinade over chicken. Refrigerate at least 4 hours or overnight.

Preheat grill to medium heat. Remove chicken from bag and discard marinade. Grill chicken using reserved marinade to baste, about 15 minutes per side or until juices run clear when pierced with fork.

Makes 4 servings.

STEEL-TOED
SIRLOIN

2 lbs. top sirloin,
 2 inches thick
Large resealable plastic bag
¼ cup frozen orange juice
 concentrate
2 Tbsp. soy sauce
2 cloves garlic, minced
1 Tbsp. fresh ginger
 or 1 tsp. ginger powder

Place sirloin in bag. Mix orange juice concentrate, soy sauce, garlic and ginger in a small bowl. Pour over meat and marinate in refrigerator at least 1 hour or overnight.

Preheat grill to medium heat. Place steak on grill and cook 8 to 10 minutes per side or until done.

Makes 4 servings.

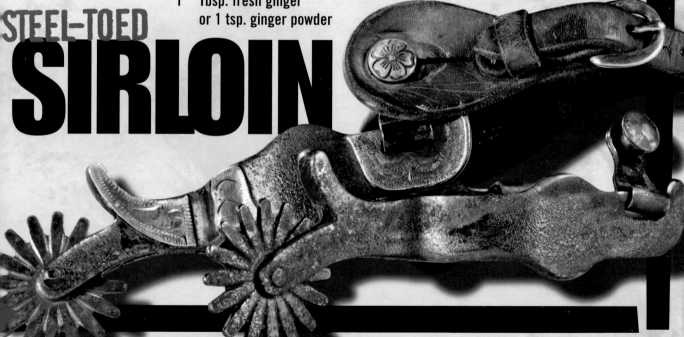

COLA NUT
SALMON

To keep the salmon from falling apart on the grill, don't remove the skin.

4   salmon fillets with or without skin

1   Tbsp. vegetable oil

½   cup chopped pecans

1   12-ounce can cola (not diet)

1   Tbsp. Tabasco® sauce

1   Tbsp. butter

Mesquite chips
(for smoking packet, see page 37)

Preheat grill to medium heat using mesquite chips.

Rinse salmon and pat dry. Brush with oil. If using skin-on fillets, cut 1-inch diagonal slits into the skin; set aside.

Toast pecans in a skillet over medium heat for 5 minutes, or until browned. Remove pecans; set aside.
Pour cola into same skillet over medium-high heat. Bring to a boil; reduce heat and simmer until cola is reduced by half and has the consistency of syrup. Stir in the Tabasco sauce, butter and pecans. Keep warm over low heat.

Grill salmon fillets, starting with the side without skin, for about 4 minutes. Carefully turn salmon over and grill for about 3 minutes, or until fish is opaque and firm to the touch; remove from grill.

To serve, spoon sauce over salmon.

Makes 4 servings.

COOKIN' ON THE COALS

Grill up great tasting sides in minutes by taking off the grate and cooking them right on the charcoal. It's easy, there's no mess and you'll look like a BBQ genius.

IMPRESS YOUR PALS— SKIP THE GRATE AND GO FOR THE FIRE.

- Always use heavy-duty aluminum foil. Store-bought heavy-duty foil bags also work well.

- Completely wrap food in a double layer of foil. Be sure not to poke any holes.

- Before cooking, spread out coals evenly.

- Be sure to turn (flip over) your foil-wrapped food often so it cooks uniformly.

- Always use heavy-duty tongs to handle food on the coals.

TRY OUT THESE SIDES WORTHY OF THE BRIQUETTES.
Or make up your own.

★ Depending on the temperature of the coals, cooking times will vary. Use these times as a guide.

CORN ON THE COB – Remove the husk, baste with melted butter and season to taste. Wrap and cook for about 15 minutes, turning every few minutes.

POTATOES – Wash well and poke several holes with a fork. Wrap and place on coals for about 30 minutes. Turn often, remove when tender.

WHOLE SWEET ONIONS – Peel away outer skin, rub on vegetable oil and sprinkle with salt, pepper and chili powder. Wrap and cook on coals for about 15 minutes. Remove when tender.

TORTILLAS – To warm 6 to 8 tortillas, wrap and place on coals for about 5 minutes. Turn once.

For extra kick, baste BBQ sauce on any of the veggies before wrapping in foil.

SWEET PEACHES

4   fresh peaches, halved, pitted or
     8 canned peach halves, drained well
Large resealable plastic bag
1   cup honey
1   Tbsp. vanilla
½   tsp. ground cinnamon
4   Tbsp. strawberry preserves,
     heated
Vanilla ice cream

Coat peaches by placing in bag with honey,
vanilla and cinnamon; refrigerate until ready
to grill. Preheat grill to medium heat. Remove
peaches from bag; reserving honey sauce.
Place on grill and cook about 2 minutes per side.

Remove from grill and spoon about 1 tablespoon strawberry
preserves into center of each peach.
Top with vanilla ice cream and reserved honey sauce.

Makes 4 servings.

APPLE
CANNONBALLS
Fire off a few at your next grillout.

¼	cup light brown sugar
¼	cup raisins
2	Tbsp. chopped nuts
½	tsp. ground cinnamon
4	large baking apples (such as Macintosh, Granny Smith or Rome)
2	Tbsp. butter, cut into quarters

Combine brown sugar, raisins, nuts and cinnamon in a small bowl; set aside. Core apples and place on individual sheets of heavy-duty aluminum foil. Spoon mixture evenly into center of each apple. Top with butter and wrap tightly in foil. Place on preheated grill and cover. Cook until tender, about 20 minutes.

Makes 4 servings.

FIRE COOK'S PORK CHOPS

8	pork chops, 1 inch thick		3	Tbsp. prepared mustard
	Large resealable plastic bag		2	Tbsp. vegetable oil
$3/4$	cup ketchup		2	Tbsp. vinegar
$3/4$	cup maple syrup		1	tsp. salt
$1/4$	cup Worcestershire sauce or steak sauce		$1/4$	tsp. ground cloves
3	Tbsp. butter		$1/4$	tsp. black pepper

Place chops in bag. Combine remaining ingredients in a small saucepan. Bring to a boil over medium heat; reduce heat and simmer 5 to 10 minutes. When cool, pour sauce over chops and refrigerate at least 2 hours or overnight. Preheat grill to medium heat.
Remove chops from bag. Grill about 25 minutes, turning and basting frequently with sauce.
Pour remaining sauce into a small saucepan. Bring to a boil over medium heat; serve with chops.

Makes 8 servings.

YOU KNOW

YOU'VE GONE TOO FAR

WHEN YOU TURN YOUR FIREPLACE

INTO A BBQ PIT.

-NOTES-

-NOTES-

INDEX

★ BIG TIME THANKS ★

Marlboro would like to tip their hat to everyone who participated, including these folks who inspired the recipes found in this book:

Gordy Ahlgren – Canby, OR

Linda Benavidez – Leslie, MI

Bach D. Chan – St. Paul, MN

Bruce Darland – Dumfries, VA

Linda Finn – Taylor, TX

Roxie Ganskop – Sioux City, IA

Wilma Howe – Houston, TX

Bonnie Huffman – Elkview, WV

Charles Hutton – Prince Frederick, MD

Wilbur Ingram – S. Euclid, OH

Joanne Kalscheur – Trevor, WI

Tanya Kissel – Peninsula, OH

Val Levey – Valencia, CA

Mark Littleton – Steger, IL

Lucas Mason – Chester, CA

Mark Morris – Las Vegas, NV

Norma Pearson – Overton, NE

Lamar Praper – Defuniak Springs, FL

Peter Quealy – Orlando, FL

Chris Retzer – East Alton, IL

Donnie Robertson – Waverly, TX

Mike Saxton – Yakima, WA

Carol Smoler – Chicago, IL

Merle Stevick – Berthold, ND

Dan Street – Rochester, NY

Pamela Turner – Evansdale, IA

Wanda Watts – London, KY

Beth Yeager – Toms River, NJ

KEEP THE COALS BURNING AND THE MEAT TURNING.